Jets

Written by
Stephen Rickard

Ransom

This is a jet.
It is quick.

This man sits in the jet.

He gets such a buzz.

This is a big jet.

It is quick as well.

The wing is long and thin.

It lets the jet be quick.

Lots of men sit in this jet.
The men will not get a buzz.

Jam the men in the jet!
This is not fun.

The jet zips up in a rush.

This man checks the jet.
Will he fix it?

No, he will not fix it. **She** will.

She will fix the wing.
She has the kit.

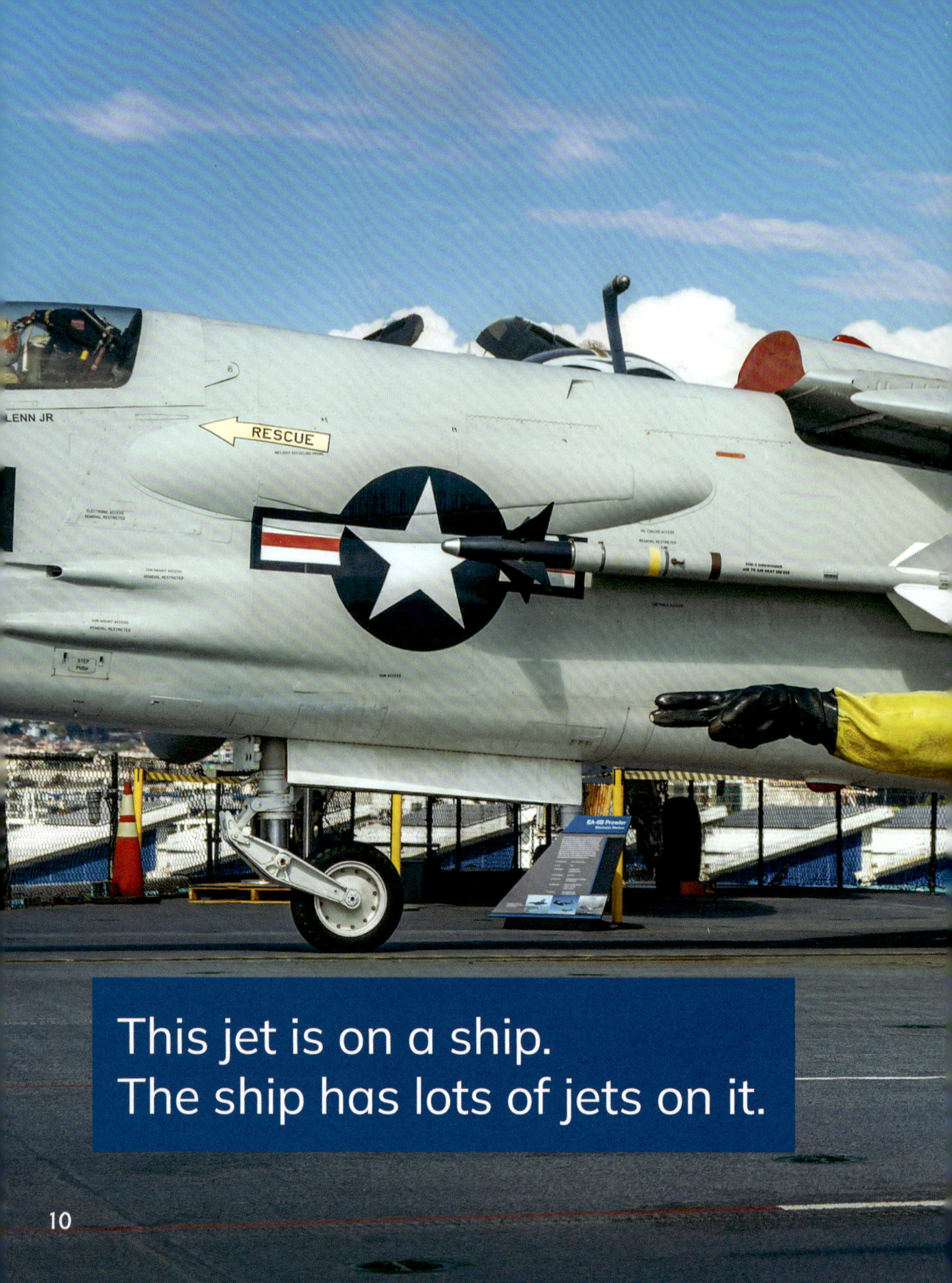

This jet is on a ship.
The ship has lots of jets on it.

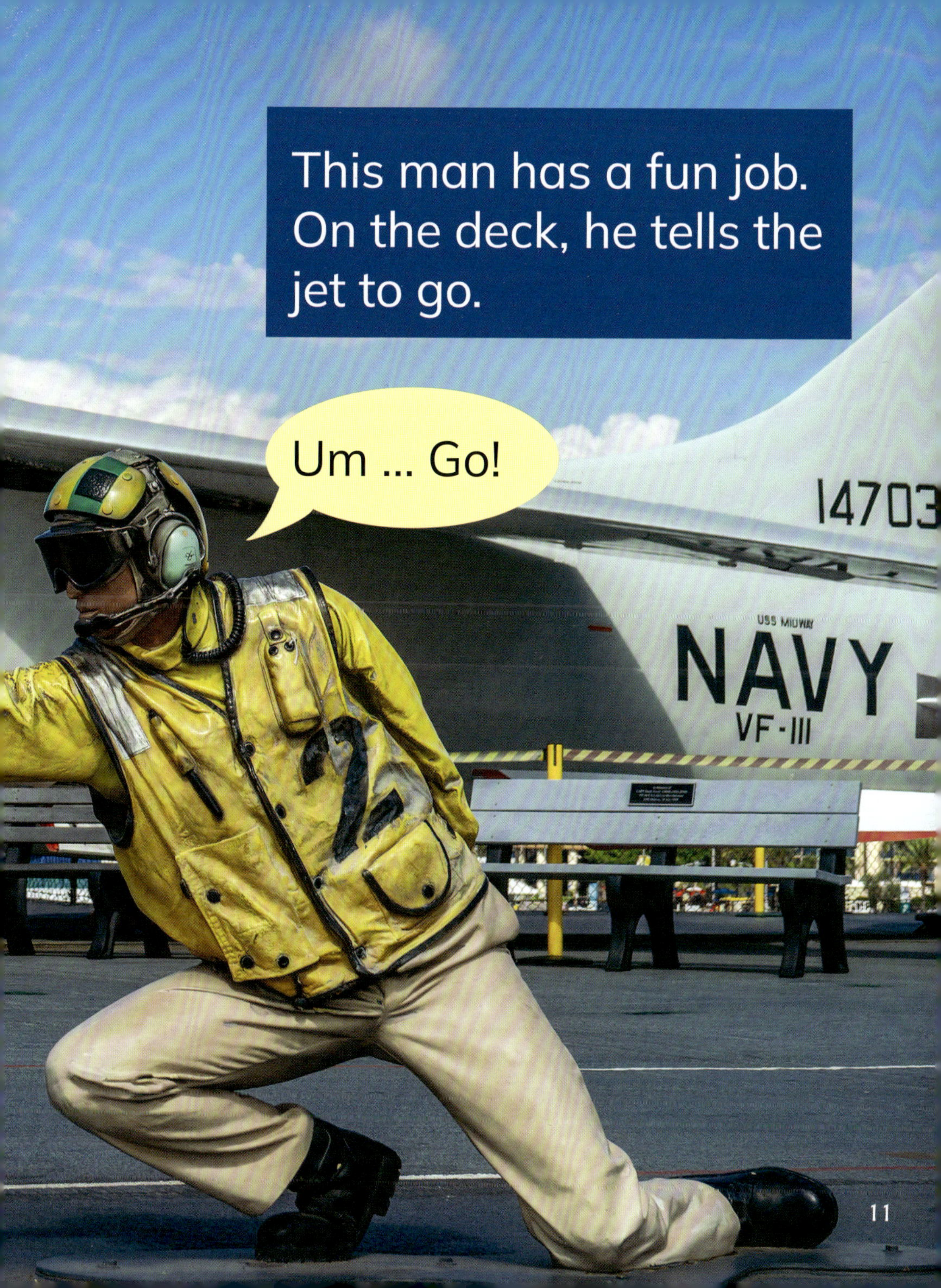
This man has a fun job.
On the deck, he tells the
jet to go.
Um ... Go!
14703
NAVY
VF-III

This is not a jet.